A Satellite of Addison-Wesley Longman

GROSSOLOGY
Begins at Home

The Science of Really Gross Things in Your Everyday Life

by Sylvia Branzei

illustrated by Jack Keely

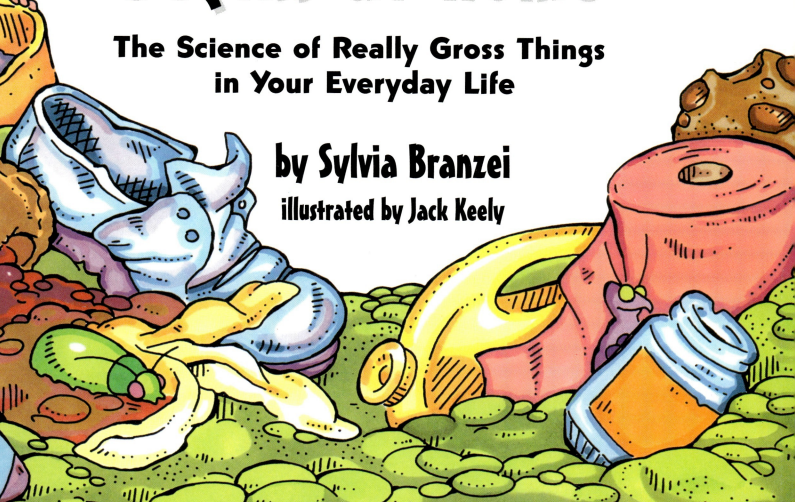

Planet Dexter and the Planet Dexter logo are registered trademarks of Addison Wesley Longman.
GROSSOLOGY is a trademark of Addison Wesley Longman.

Many of the designations used by manufacturers and sellers to distinguish their products are claimed as trademarks. Where those designations appear in this book and Addison Wesley Longman was aware of a trademark claim, the designations have been printed with initial capital letters.

ISBN 0-201-95993-3
Copyright © 1997 by Sylvia Branzei
Illustrations © 1997 by Jack Keely

This book is dedicated to Dave's 1996 Whale Gulch Junior High School Class: Aia, Ari, Bryant, Leeann, Lexie, Nessa, Serina, Summer, Thomas, William, and Zoe. My greatest critics and a source of much inspiration.

Cover design by C. Shane Sykes
Interior design by C. Shane Sykes and Jack Keely
Illustrated by Jack Keely

Set in various sizes of Grizzly, Gill Sans, and Mister Earl.

2 3 4 5 6 7 8 9 -GC- 00999897
Second printing, November 1997

Through the Addison Wesley Longman TRIΔNGLE Program, Planet Dexter books are available FROM YOUR BOOKSELLER at special discounts for bulk purchases; or contact the Corporate, Government, and Special Sales Department at Addison Wesley Longman, One Jacob Way, Reading, MA 01867; or call (800) 238-9682.

The Planet Dexter Guarantee

If for any reason you are not satisfied with this book, please send a simple note
telling us why (how else will we be able to make our future books better?!) along with the book to:

The Editors of Planet Dexter
One Jacob Way
Reading, MA 01867-3999

We'll read your note carefully, and send back to you a free copy of another Planet Dexter book. And we'll keep doing that until we find the perfect Planet Dexter book for you.

Cool, eh?

Pssst! A tip:
Visit
grossology.com
on the world
wide web.

AND NOW A MESSAGE FROM OUR CORPORATE LAWYER:

"Neither the Publisher nor the Author shall be liable for any damage that may be caused or sustained as a result of conducting any of the activities in this book without specifically following instructions, conducting the activities without proper supervision, or ignoring the cautions contained in the book."

The GROSStents of Your Home

Your Home Is Gross It's True

(AN INTRODUCTION)

There's a whole world of grossness right under your nose, your eyes, and your feet. Just when you thought you were safe, grossology moved in. Yep, nowhere is sacred for a grossologist. And your home is the perfect laboratory for the science of really putrid things.

Take a tour of your little house of grossness. Around every corner is a yucky discovery. In every nook and cranny is a disgusting surprise. Even your body is home to invisible, icky creatures. Face it. There's no use hiding. There's no escape. You can't run or fight it. Grossology begins at home.

Just think, once you master the stuff in this book, you can really upset your friends and relatives when you say things like, "Did you know there are little bacteria swimming all over the counter?" and "The flushing of a toilet sends a fine mist of pee pee all over the bathroom. Maybe you should move the toothbrushes to the cupboard."

During a single day, you encounter gobs of sickening things. Most of the time, you overlook them. Now it is time to embrace them! To truly love the foul in your life!

Let go, and let grossology in.

Dust Mites and Friends

THEY'RE EVERYWHERE

They're all after you. Run! A slimy, brown glob almost gets your heels, but you pull it away. Oh no! It's a furry green stringy creature. **Yuck!** You swerve to escape, just in time. The ground becomes covered in crunchy crawling things. **Ick!** You can't get away. They are everywhere. **Help!**

Your eyes pop open and adjust. Yes, it was only a dream. Not real at all. You swipe the eye gunk from the corners of your eyes. Yep, it's just another gross day. **Gross day?** Well, you never know what you'll come across. You stretch, then shudder as you recall the nightmare—brown slimies, green furries, and millions of crunchies. You check under the covers. **Nope, just you.**

Wow, it's great to lie in your bed, alone. Actually, you just *think* that you are by yourself. You are not alone at all.

At this moment, beneath you, hidden in your mattress, are millions of teensy, eight-legged creatures. As you read these words, they are under you—feasting, mating, birthing, dying, and pooping. **Ack!**

Maybe you should move to your overstuffed chair. No good. They are there as well. *How about the carpet?* Nope. The carpet is home to millions more. *A wooden chair at a rarely-used desk?* Maybe, except that dust is partly composed of the corpses and fecal matter of these little armored critters, which are closely related to ticks, spiders, and scorpions. *The recently washed tile floor in the kitchen?* Now you're thinking, but you may as well give up. Dust mites are found in almost 100% of all homes. They are also present anywhere with stuffed furniture, carpet, or dust. Vacuum cleaner bags are a most favorite spot.

Dust mites are so tiny several hundred could live comfortably on a flea. Their small size explains why they weren't even discovered until 1967. (Maybe you would prefer it if they never had been discovered at all.)

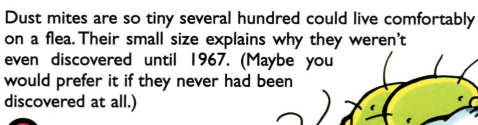

Mitey Poopy

About 42,000 dust mites live in each ounce of mattress dust and each of these mites pinches out about 20 poops every day. Think about that the next time you climb into your comfortable bed.

Where to Meet a Mite
A perfect home for dust mites is your vacuum cleaner bag. Yummy skin flakes abound. When scientists who study the little critters need to repopulate their supply, they go home and give the house a quick cleaning.

Dust mites really aren't too cute according to human standards. They resemble a candy-covered peanut with eight legs and two claws. Little rakes are attached to one side of the claws for shoveling in food. Dust mite bodies are covered with armor plates and stubby hairs. They have no eyes, ears, or nose. Little holes serve for eating, breathing, pooping, and reproducing. Magnified thousands of times, they look like creatures featured in science fiction films or in nightmares.

Actually, the homely little creatures don't hurt you. They are docile animals that hang around grazing all day. However, they don't graze on grass; they collect and eat your scaling skin.

"Gee, Mom. Not skin flakes, again."

Yep, your dead skin is another creature's bread and butter. Each day billions of skin flakes rub off of your body. Lots of them come off while you sleep at night. The dust mites hang out and wait for the flakes to rain down upon them. With the little rakes on their claws, the dust mites shovel in your skin scales. The weeks-long life of a dust mite is pretty simple—be born, eat skin scales, poop, maybe crawl around a little, reproduce, eat skin scales, poop, die.

OK, I take it back. There is one way that dust mites can harm people. That is with their dead corpses and their fecal waste. Often people who have allergies to dust are actually reacting to the dust mite remains. Mite-free homes often belong to dust allergy sufferers, as many precautions are taken to rid the house of all dust.

But even if you're standing on a cold, clean tile floor, you can't really get away from mites.

They are always with you, very with you, because some mites live . . . on your body!

9

ON MY BODY?

Yep, right under your nose in the hairs on your upper lip, right in front of your eyes in your eyelashes, and in your ears.

About **one in 10** Americans has mites hanging on his or her eyelashes. These wormy mites are called **follicle (FALL ick ull)** mites. Follicles are the places on your skin where a hair grows out. A follicle is the little hole at the base of the hair. Your whole body is covered with follicles.

Eyelash follicle mites choose to live in only one type of hair hole—the ones at the base of your eyelashes. Boy, are they picky about where they live or what? The long-bodied creatures spend their days with their heads down in the roots of the eyelashes. They only leave the base of the eyelash at night as you sleep. Nighttime is the right time for eyelash mites to seek out another mite for mating or to find a new location on another eyelash. Nope, they don't come off with soap and water. Nope, eye makeup does not smother them; they rather like the greasy stuff.

Since not everyone has them, you might figure that you are not home to the swiggly follicle mites. **Well, you're right:** You may not have them in your eyelashes. But other types of follicle mites live on the hairs on your upper lip or in your eyebrows. There is even one type of mite that lives in the oil glands on your face. The oil-gland type are loners compared to the hair mites, since they live only one mite to an oil gland.

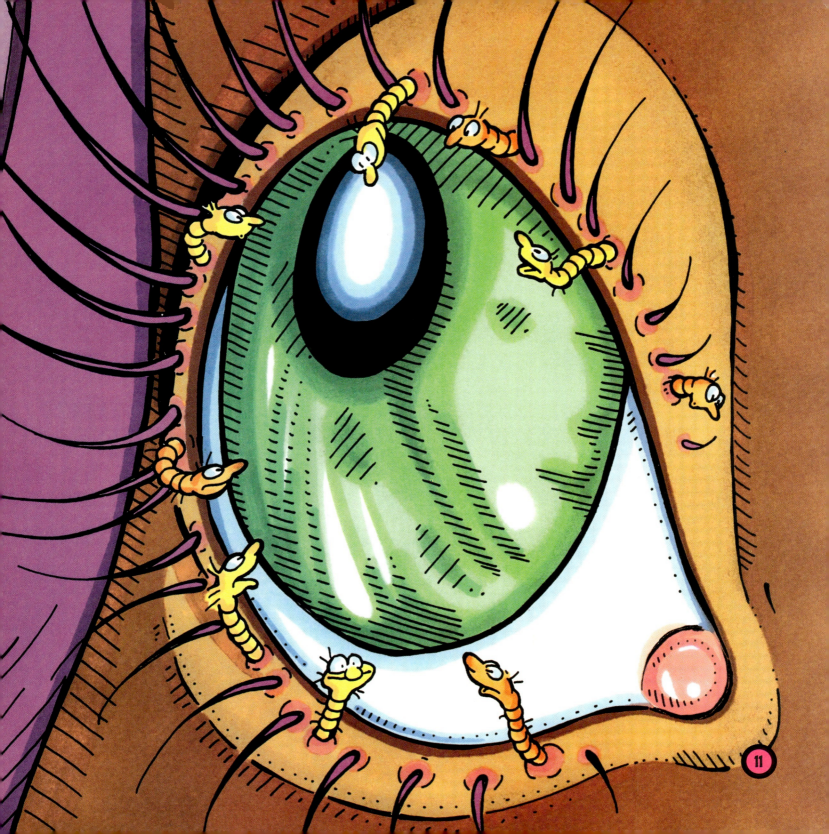

Face it! Your mug is home to at least one of the friendly-but-creepy mite families.

So, right now the mites are hanging out, or rather hanging on to, your face. They are mating and laying eggs right on your lovely mug.

Oh, ack! *They are probably pooping all over it, too!*

Actually, no. It turns out that follicle mites do not have buttholes. Basically, they die at a young age because they suffer from constant constipation. Poor critters. Even if they are not leaving waste, they are right now on your face—eating, mating, being born, and dying.

Even if you shaved off all of the hair on your face, the follicle mites would still be there. Although you would no longer have hairs protruding from the follicle openings, the mites' cave homes are still on your face.

You shudder at the thought of the mites climbing about in your bed and upon your face. "But what the hey, mites are my friends," you tell yourself. You repeat the mantra, "Mites are my friends, mites are my friends." You slip off into slumber land once again.

Ode to the Mighty Mite
Dust mite, dust mite in my bed,
You feast upon my skin that's dead.
Although you don't bite or make me itch,
You do make my ACHOOO nose twitch.

Face mite, face mite in my pore,
I wash until my skin is sore.
But you eat and mate and stay in place.
At least you don't poop upon my face.

Dog Breath
Why it Stinks

While in a peaceful slumber, you dream about eating popcorn. The giant bowl of freshly-made goodies is placed before you. A moist warmth greets your face. You lean over the huge bowl to take a great whiff.

Ack! Putrid!

Your eyes pop open, another dream shattered. A huge, gaping, panting mouth hurls hot, wet, stinky air into your nose. "Yuck, Rufus. Git outta here." Your not-so-happy greeting makes his tail wag even faster and his rancid breath moves even closer to your face for a lick. **"Oh no! Dog breath attack!"**

If you told Rover he had bad breath, he really wouldn't care. Dogs just don't seem to notice that kind of thing. In fact, when two dogs meet, they often share a brief breath-smelling moment. The breath check tells each dog what the other one last nibbled upon. "Golly Buddy, where'd ya put the bone?" "Hey, how about you, Sox? Smells like you found a great garbage can."

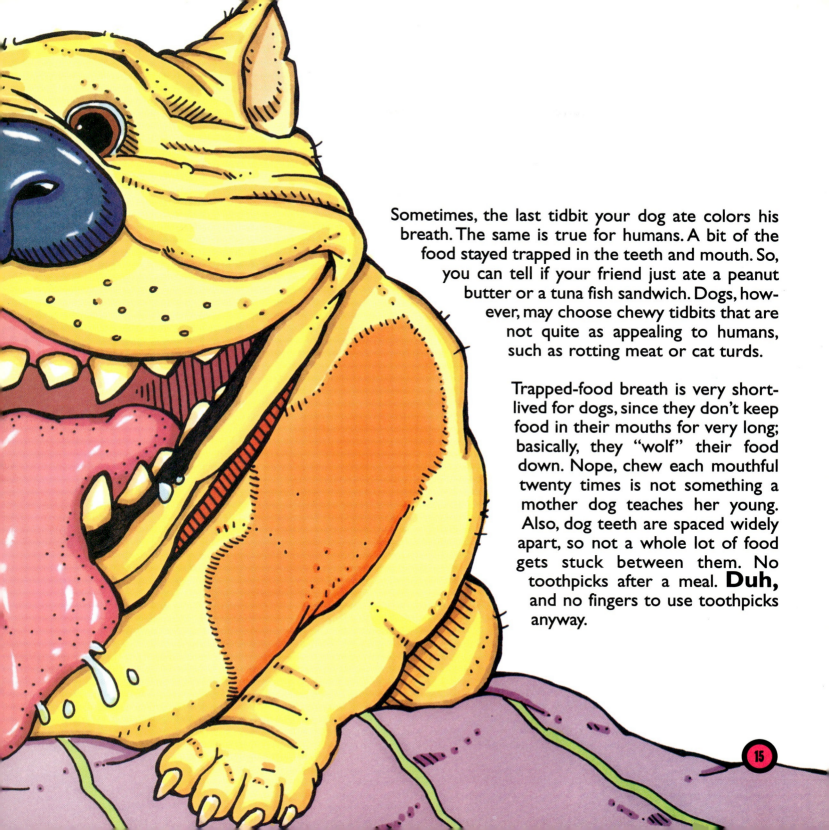

Sometimes, the last tidbit your dog ate colors his breath. The same is true for humans. A bit of the food stayed trapped in the teeth and mouth. So, you can tell if your friend just ate a peanut butter or a tuna fish sandwich. Dogs, however, may choose chewy tidbits that are not quite as appealing to humans, such as rotting meat or cat turds.

Trapped-food breath is very short-lived for dogs, since they don't keep food in their mouths for very long; basically, they "wolf" their food down. Nope, chew each mouthful twenty times is not something a mother dog teaches her young. Also, dog teeth are spaced widely apart, so not a whole lot of food gets stuck between them. No toothpicks after a meal. **Duh,** and no fingers to use toothpicks anyway.

Another short-term cause of foul doggie breath is an upset stomach. Many dogs are not very particular about what they eat. Decayed food in the compost pile is a wonderful treat. Or a moldy sandwich under your bed is a yummy find. Although a dog's digestive system can handle a lot more disgusting foods than a human stomach, there are limits. Champ's midnight chomping can cause a slight belly ache. You only notice his upset stomach when he gives you a big slobbery kiss. A doggie belly ache should last only a day. If the disgusting breath lingers, take Champ to the vet.

Fe Fe must always have a belly ache, because her breath is constantly gross. If your dog is in continuous need of breath mints, check her teeth.

Pant, Pant, Pant
Puppy breath is very interesting (actually, some people might say that it smells downright awful). Puppy breath lasts until the milk teeth are replaced by permanent teeth. This occurs in about six months.

WARNING:
Don't try this on dogs that you don't know really well.

If you notice brown stains, she may have tartar build-up. Yep, just like humans, dogs get tartar. Dogs chew on most anything. And most anything has bacteria on it. The bacteria get in the dog's mouth. Foreign bacteria coupled with resident bacteria live and die and make waste in Fe Fe's mouth. Bacteria stuff and putrefying food bits cement to your dog's teeth with the help of your dog's spit, or saliva. Whala! Bad doggie breath.

Yucky breath is more common in some types of dogs. Boston terriers, bulldogs, pugs, Chihuahuas, and miniature poodles have a problem with tartar build-up because of teeth crowding. Also, dogs that eat only canned or squishy dog food build up tartar more quickly because Pepe doesn't have to crunch away. Hard kibbles actually help to clean a dog's teeth.

Grrrrrrrrrr The large hooked teeth, or fangs, in your mouth and in your dog's mouth, are called canine teeth. Canine also refers to the entire dog family. In humans, the canine teeth are sometimes referred to as eye teeth. Seems dog teeth would be more accurate.

So, you checked Fang's teeth, you didn't get bit, and you know she has tartar. What do you do now? If it is not too bad, give her nylon chew bones and hard biscuits. The gnawing action may help. You can also brush her teeth.

Wait—did you say 'brush her teeth'?

Well, since she doesn't have fingers, she can't do it herself. Doggie tooth care may take a while for you and Fido to get used to, so start off slowly. Do not use human toothpaste, as Fido will spit it out. Start by rubbing one tooth with a moist cloth. (If Killer doesn't like having her teeth rubbed, don't push it.) Then, over several days, try more and more teeth. Rub along the gum where the tartar builds up. Give Fido a treat after each dental event. After a while, you can try using a cloth with doggie toothpaste or a little bit of baking soda. Make sure he rinses with water to get the cleaner out. If your dog decides this is great fun, you can graduate to a toothbrush. Brush doggie's teeth once a week for a clean and refreshing mouth.

If there's a gob of tartar build-up, you can take Ginger to the vet for a professional cleaning. No, do not take dogs to a people dentist; they don't sit well in the chairs.

Thanks to Rufus, you are very awake. Rufus leaps from your bed and bounds out the door. Only the lingering memory of her breath remains. Guess it's time to get out of bed. But get out of bed to do what?

Toe Jam

PRETTY MUCH AS GROSS AS IT SOUNDS

You look around your room. Yep, it's the same as you left it before you went to sleep, before that horrible nightmare. Nothing to do. At least, nothing interesting to do. "Guess I'll do what I always do at a time like this—play with my toes."

You plop down upon the floor and remove the toenail clipper from the chest by your bed. Guess it was a while since you last played with your toes. Your toenails are really long.

As you peacefully trim your toenails, you notice the disgusting stinky stuff under them. Toe jam! (Toe jam includes both the stuff between the toes and under the toenails.)

**"This stuff is gross.
I wonder what toe jam really is?"**

When you take off your shoes and socks after a long day, you might swipe it from between your toes. It is usually a grayish color and it smells pretty nasty. Spread it on bread and add some crushed peanuts and you have a peanut butter and toe jam sandwich.

Yummy.

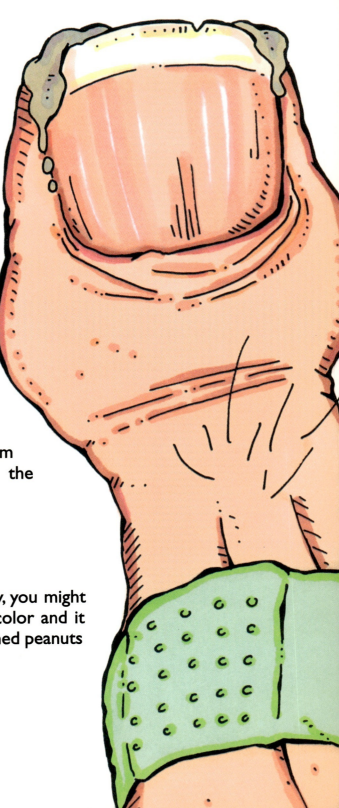

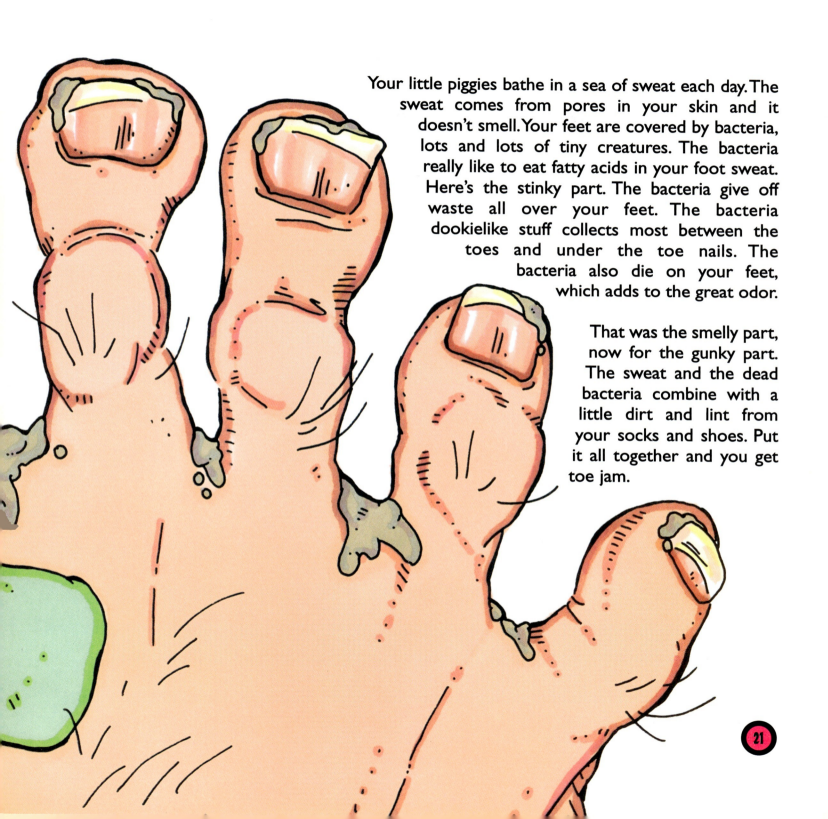

Your little piggies bathe in a sea of sweat each day. The sweat comes from pores in your skin and it doesn't smell. Your feet are covered by bacteria, lots and lots of tiny creatures. The bacteria really like to eat fatty acids in your foot sweat. Here's the stinky part. The bacteria give off waste all over your feet. The bacteria dookielike stuff collects most between the toes and under the toe nails. The bacteria also die on your feet, which adds to the great odor.

That was the smelly part, now for the gunky part. The sweat and the dead bacteria combine with a little dirt and lint from your socks and shoes. Put it all together and you get toe jam.

21

If you inspect the toe jam under your tootsie's nail, you will notice it is a bit more crusty than the stuff between your little piggies. Each day a person who weighs about 80 pounds shoves more than **200 tons** of pressure onto each foot. Imagine lifting 33 elephants that each weight about 6 tons every single day. That is how much pressure you pound on your poor feet daily. When you walk, the tips of your toes cram into the front of your shoe. The push of your toes against the front of your shoe shoves toe jam ingredients under your toenail. The stuff builds up under the nail. It becomes compact and more crusty. So, nail toe jam is just toe jam all crammed together into a chunk.

Toe jam won't hurt you, but it can make your feet really stinky. The real answer to toe jam is, don't wear shoes. Barefoot or even sandaled feet don't allow the sweat to stick around, so bacteria don't grow. So the toe jam is mostly caked-up dirt and skin cells. It's much less stinky, though still disgusting.

Since not wearing shoes or wearing sandals all the time is not really possible for most of us, you should wash your feet regularly and trim your toenails. Caution! Caution! Don't trim your toenails like little half moons. Cut them straight across. If you curve the edges, you might end up with a painful ingrown toenail. But that's a whole other gross topic.

You replace the clipper in the drawer. As you admire your preened little piggies, an uncomfortable feeling draws your attention, a feeling of being very full. You know what it means, so you clamber from your bed.

Toilets

EVERYTHING YOU WERE AFRAID TO ASK

You race down the hallway. "I hope no one beat me to this very special room." You reach the vacated bathroom just in time. You have to go so bad, you can barely stand it.

Ahhhhhhhhhh! The tinkle of relief.

After you pee pee or dookie in the bowl, you probably just flush it away and don't even think about it. Unless you leave a really stinking one—then you might remember it for a couple of minutes.

Well, there's a whole lot more to the toilet thing than flush, flush.

First, the act of flushing causes the water in the bowl to swirl around. The mixing water sends a light mist into the bathroom. Yep, that mist has little tiny droplets of pee in it. Maybe even a couple of poo poo molecules. If your toothbrush sits out in the open, the mist settles upon it.

Yuck!

And the pee and poop isn't all. Some of the droplets might contain tiny bacteria or viruses. Scientists estimated that more than 60,000 contaminated droplets could be released after one flush. The disease-causing drops float around in the air for several hours, then fall to land on the wall, the faucet, the toilet paper, and pretty much everywhere. The critters will live for several days in their little bubble. If you touch a microbe-filled bubble, you may get sick.

So, should I stop flushing? Nope, simply wash your hands after you flush. Just like your mommy told you.

24

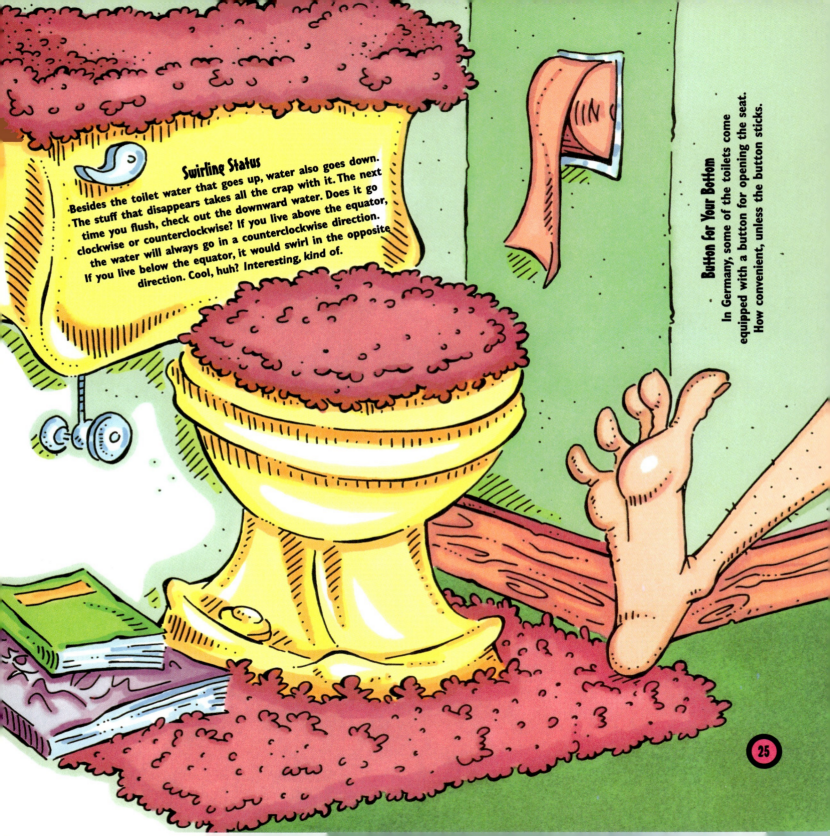

Swirling Status

Besides the toilet water that goes up, water also goes down. The stuff that disappears takes all the crap with it. The next time you flush, check out the downward water. Does it go clockwise or counterclockwise? If you live above the equator, the water will always go in a counterclockwise direction. If you live below the equator, it would swirl in the opposite direction. Cool, huh? Interesting, kind of.

Button for Your Bottom

In Germany, some of the toilets come equipped with a button for opening the seat. How convenient, unless the button sticks.

25

On Your Marks, Get Set, Go!
For a great time, attend the toilet races in Montreal, Canada. The students at Concordia University make elaborate toilet-mobiles. The rolling toilets race complete with a crapper upon the seat.

After the swirling water is carried away, it combines with other wastewater, such as the water from the dirty dishes, the laundry, and the shower. **Hey, it's a great big wastewater party!**

If you live in a city or town, your wastewater combines with the crud water from all over the area. Hey, it's an even bigger wastewater party! The dirty water flows through pipes until it reaches a wastewater treatment plant. Also known as a poo poo factory by a select few people.

First the yucky water goes into a huge settling tank at the plant. In the tank, the big stuff like poo, toilet paper, ground up food, and dirt goes to the bottom of the tank. The crud on the bottom is called sludge. The sludge is scraped from the tank and sent to digester tanks. Bacteria await the sludge. They love the stuff and they eagerly eat it up.

"Uga! Sludge, my favorite. Burp. Fart."

The bacteria burp and fart so much that most of the sludge is changed into carbon dioxide and methane gas. The carbon dioxide is released into the air and the fart gas, methane, is used to power the treatment plant. The sludge is now called mixed liquor. The liquid from the mixed liquor is removed for further treatment and then released into local rivers and lakes or used to water golf courses and highway landscaping. It is about **95% clean.** The bacteria is removed from the heavy crud. It is then used for plant fertilizer. And you thought your turds just disappeared when you pulled the handle.

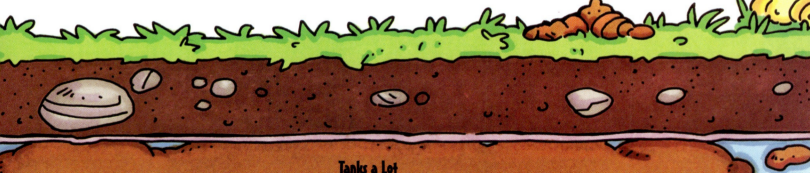

Tanks a Lot
Not everyone's dookie gets to go to the big party at the treatment plant. Some rural people have septic tanks that serve as mini-treatment plants. The big difference is that the water just flows into the ground. This works out fine, as long as the well for the drinking water is far away from the septic tank. If it's not, don't ask for a drink of water when you visit. The sludge is pumped out periodically. Yep, and you, too, can have a job pumping sludge out of septic tanks.

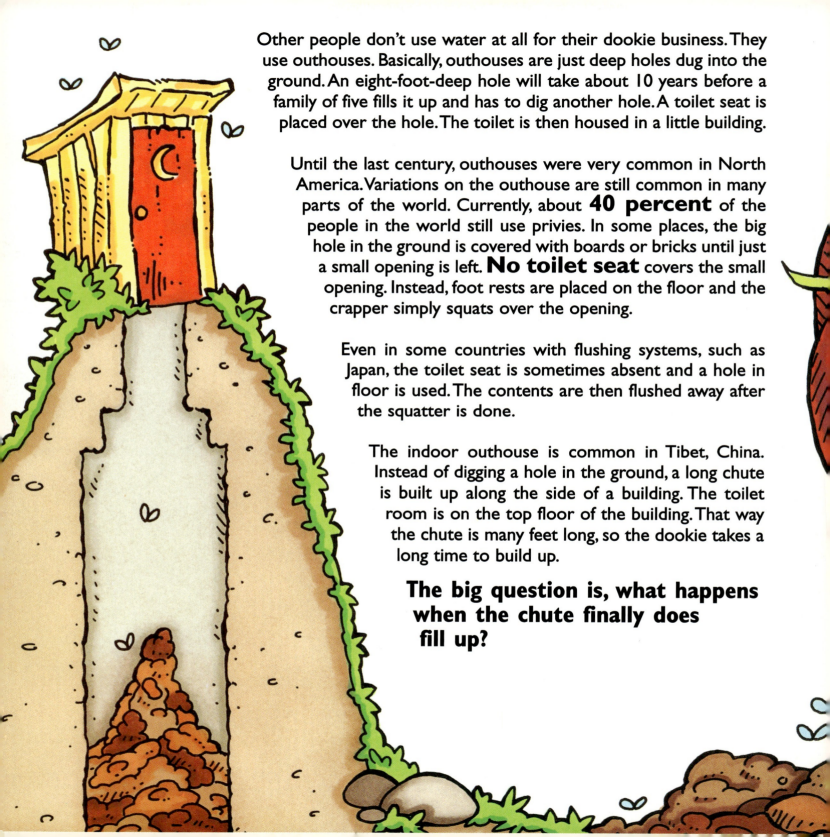

Other people don't use water at all for their dookie business. They use outhouses. Basically, outhouses are just deep holes dug into the ground. An eight-foot-deep hole will take about 10 years before a family of five fills it up and has to dig another hole. A toilet seat is placed over the hole. The toilet is then housed in a little building.

Until the last century, outhouses were very common in North America. Variations on the outhouse are still common in many parts of the world. Currently, about **40 percent** of the people in the world still use privies. In some places, the big hole in the ground is covered with boards or bricks until just a small opening is left. **No toilet seat** covers the small opening. Instead, foot rests are placed on the floor and the crapper simply squats over the opening.

Even in some countries with flushing systems, such as Japan, the toilet seat is sometimes absent and a hole in floor is used. The contents are then flushed away after the squatter is done.

The indoor outhouse is common in Tibet, China. Instead of digging a hole in the ground, a long chute is built up along the side of a building. The toilet room is on the top floor of the building. That way the chute is many feet long, so the dookie takes a long time to build up.

The big question is, what happens when the chute finally does fill up?

Useful Dookie

A high tech solution to outhouses is the composting toilet. This toilet uses no water, is indoors, and turns the poops into fertilizer. Some people choose these toilets for their get-away cabins. A few other odd people use them in their homes. The toilet has a seat on top but underneath is a drum, or storage area. Instead of using water to flush away the mass, peat moss is dumped down the hole after every use. Air, bacteria, and peat moss change the urine and feces into fertilizer. When it is time to remove the glob of human waste, it doesn't smell like poofume at all. It smells like dirt. That's because that's what it is. The fertilizer can then be used in the garden. Most people believe that the transformed dookie should not be used for food that grows underground, but in China human waste is a common source of fertilizer for the field crops. So, who knows? One sure thing: the composting toilet doesn't waste water, or even waste waste.

Up the Poop Chute

Back in the days of kings and queens and castles, poop chutes like those found in Tibet were common. If a castle came under attack, the poop chute became a perfect entrance into the castle. Pity the poor soldier who got that assignment. The poop chutes were later removed because they became such a prime place for enemy infiltration. Wow! That's what you really call getting attacked from the behind.

No matter if you flush it, dump it, or peat moss it, you also need to wipe it away. Toilet paper is the wiper of choice for many people. But it has only been around for a little over a hundred years. Toilet paper wasn't invented until 1879 by the Scott Brothers. And people didn't flock to buy it, either. Basically, it seemed like a waste of money when you could use old catalogs or the newspaper. Who cares if a little ink rubbed off on your butt? No paper around? Leaves or an old cloth would do.

Actually, toilet paper is not available in all of the world, so the old methods still work. In certain developing countries, people simply use their hands for wiping. Some cultures have taught people to eat with the right hand because the left hand was for wiping.

If you squat, though, there usually isn't anything to wipe. Think about your dog and your cat. The squatting thing really works. Some people claim our bodies were actually designed to relieve themselves in a squat. But since many of us have chosen to sit, we need toilet paper. So, the next time you sit upon the throne, think about the wondrous toilet.

With great relief, you finish your business and reach out to push down the handle. From the corner of your eye, you spy your toothbrush next to the sink. You hesitate, think twice, then close the lid before flushing. Swoosh.

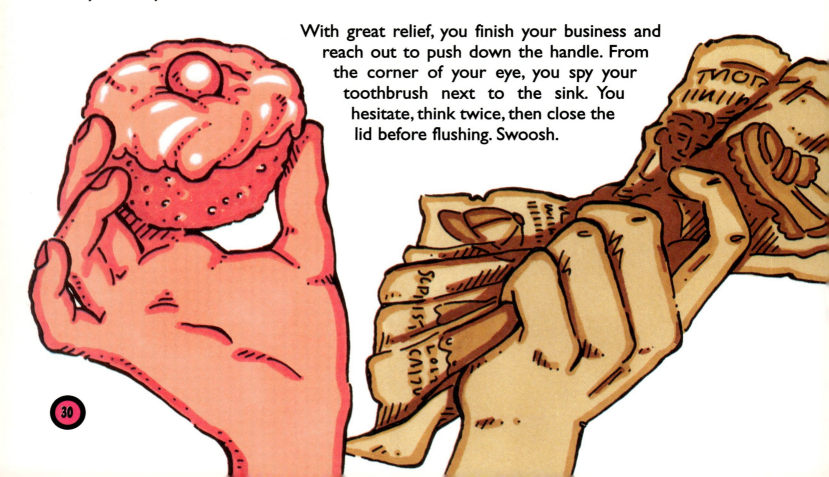

Toilet Paper Testing

WHAT YOU NEED:

Several brands of toilet paper, water, dropper, a dozen large nuts or bolts.

WHAT YOU DO:

To test for absorbency, remove three squares from each brand of toilet paper. For each brand, fold the squares along the perforations to make one square. You should now have one square that is three layers thick. Use the dropper to place one drop of water on each of the brands. Check the bottom layer of each brand to see if the water leaked through. Add water drop by drop to each brand until one leaks. The first one to leak is the least absorbent. The one that hold the most drops before leaking is the most absorbent.

To test for strength, remove one square from each brand. Wet the center of each square. Place one nut or bolt on each square. Lift. Do any of the brands rip? Add nuts or bolts until one of the brands rips when lifted. The brand to rip first is the least strong, the one to rip last is the most strong.

Cavities

A ROTTEN SITUATION

Now it is time for another modern convenience of health care. You retrieve your toothbrush and toothpaste. You squeeze the chalk-paint-detergent stuff onto your toothbrush, then place it to your teeth.

In the time of the ancient Greeks, a doctor by the name of Hippocrates told his patients they should grind up marble and use it to brush their teeth. His suggestion wasn't very popular.

If you hate going to the dentist, you might wish that you lived before dentists existed. Actually, if you lived thousands of years ago, you probably wouldn't even need a dentist. Skulls found in graves thousands of years old have fine sets of teeth. These teeth are worn, but the owner could boast, **"Look Ma, no cavities!"**

What? Were cavities not invented yet? No, sugar and sugary foods were not invented yet. Thousands of years ago, sugar was only available in fruits and honey. Once sugar was grown, ground, and gobbled up, cavities came into the picture. Even today, in countries where people eat little sugar, their teeth stay healthy even when they are very old.

Hey! *I don't eat candy, but I still have cavities.* Saliva is the culprit. Yep, good old spit or saliva. Saliva breaks down carbohydrates like bread, noodles, and crackers to form sugar.

Actually, it's not exactly the sugar that causes cavities, it's the acid. *ACID? People don't go around sucking on car batteries, so how does acid get into mouths?* Just as you like to eat sugary things, so does the bacteria, or microcreatures, that live in your mouth. One type of ball-shaped bacteria, called *Streptococcus Mutans*, is especially fond of sugar and sugar from starch. When you eat sweets, the tiny leftovers stick to your teeth. And for the bacteria it's,

"All right! More sugar, my favorite!"
The beasties chomp on the microsweets and produce acid.

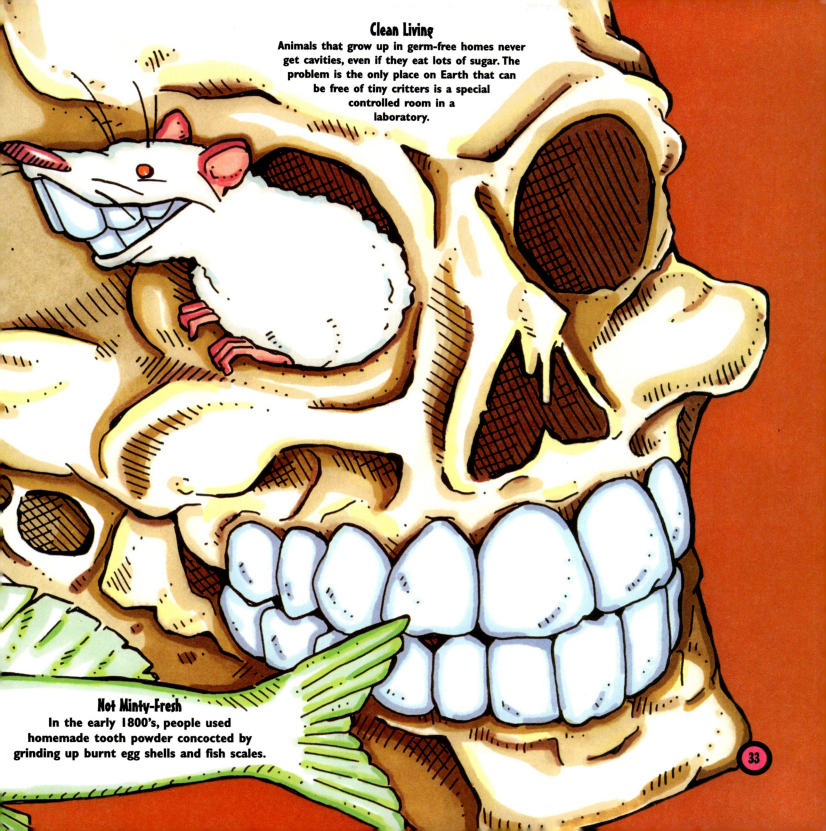

Clean Living
Animals that grow up in germ-free homes never get cavities, even if they eat lots of sugar. The problem is the only place on Earth that can be free of tiny critters is a special controlled room in a laboratory.

Not Minty-Fresh
In the early 1800's, people used homemade tooth powder concocted by grinding up burnt egg shells and fish scales.

33

The tiny amounts of acid that the bacteria spit out after a sugary meal attacks the hardest part of your body—tooth enamel. The acid is so strong that it forms little holes. The little holes turn into craters. Once the attack begins it can't be stopped, unless you go to the dentist.

The dentist removes the infected, crusty, decaying, disgusting area of the tooth. The tooth fixer does this with a high-speed whining drill. The drill rotates about **100,000** times each minute. Imagine the sound and the smell of a dental drill wearing at your tooth. Did the thought make your jaws tense or your mouth water? After the awful portion of the tooth is removed, it is filled with metal or plastic. Once the hole is filled, you can go home.

The most common question that is probably asked after someone visits the dentist is "How many cavities did you have?" If you follow these anticavity rules, you may be able to answer, "None."

1. **Brush you teeth really well after meals and snacks.**

2. **Use dental floss to get into the hard to reach places.**

3. **Don't eat lots and lots of sweets.**

You spit out the saliva-filled toothpaste, then swish your mouth. After a quick wash, you're ready to face the day. Or are you? As you replace the tube of toothpaste in the cabinet, you notice something new in the bathroom cabinet. **Something gross.**

You reach into the cabinet . . .

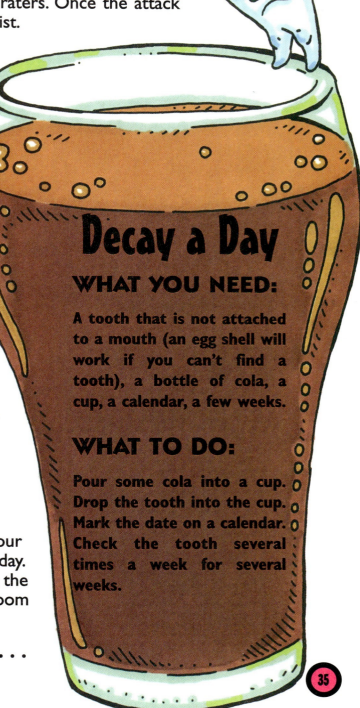

Decay a Day

WHAT YOU NEED:

A tooth that is not attached to a mouth (an egg shell will work if you can't find a tooth), a bottle of cola, a cup, a calendar, a few weeks.

WHAT TO DO:

Pour some cola into a cup. Drop the tooth into the cup. Mark the date on a calendar. Check the tooth several times a week for several weeks.

Hemorrhoids

NOT PILES OF FUN

From the bathroom cabinet, you pull out a tube of hemorrhoid cream. You close the cabinet door, look in the mirror, hold up the tube, and quote from the television commercial, "For relief from the pain, itching, and burning caused by hemorrhoids . . ." You look at the tube in disgust. "Yuck! Euooh! Hemorrhoids!" You definitely know that you don't want them. "But what are hemorrhoids?"

Hemorrhoids (HEM a royds) are swollen veins in the bootie. Hemorrhoids are also called piles. They only occur in humans. It must have been a strange job going around looking at the buttholes of different animal species to find out that fact.

Actually, there are two types of hemorrhoids. Piles located inside the butthole area are called internal hemorrhoids. Piles that develop under the skin at the entrance of the butthole are called external hemorrhoids. These external piles can even be seen as purple or blue lumps around the anal opening.

TP to the Rescue
In 1885, some people were convinced that chemically treated toilet paper was the answer to their pile problems. The ad for the toilet tissue said that regular use would assure permanent relief.

36

Some medical experts estimate that over 90 percent of the people who live in modern societies get hemorrhoids at one time or another. That's almost everyone. But hemorrhoids are most common in people over 50 years old and in pregnant women. It is usually easy to tell if you have piles. When you poop, it hurts, and you may find blood on the toilet paper after you wipe. When you aren't on the toilet, your butthole itches and burns. **Not fun!**

Like cookies and milk, hemorrhoids and constipation, or not being able to poop, go together. And a diet with a lot of cookies and milk and other refined foods can be the cause of this rear end problem.

When food is digested, it collects in the last part of the colon, or the end of the large intestine. Here the body usually stores poop, or **feces (FEE cees)**, until you let it go in the toilet. If the poo doesn't have a lot of fiber or bulk, it stays in the colon. Since the poop stays in the colon longer than usual, water continues to draw away. The turd becomes compact and hard instead.

At the toilet, the hardened poop doesn't come out easily. The crapper has to push and strain. The pressure from the pushing weakens the veins under the skin and they become swollen to form hemorrhoids. The hard feces scrape past the swollen veins to pull them downward. This may cause the hemorrhoids to exit the butthole.

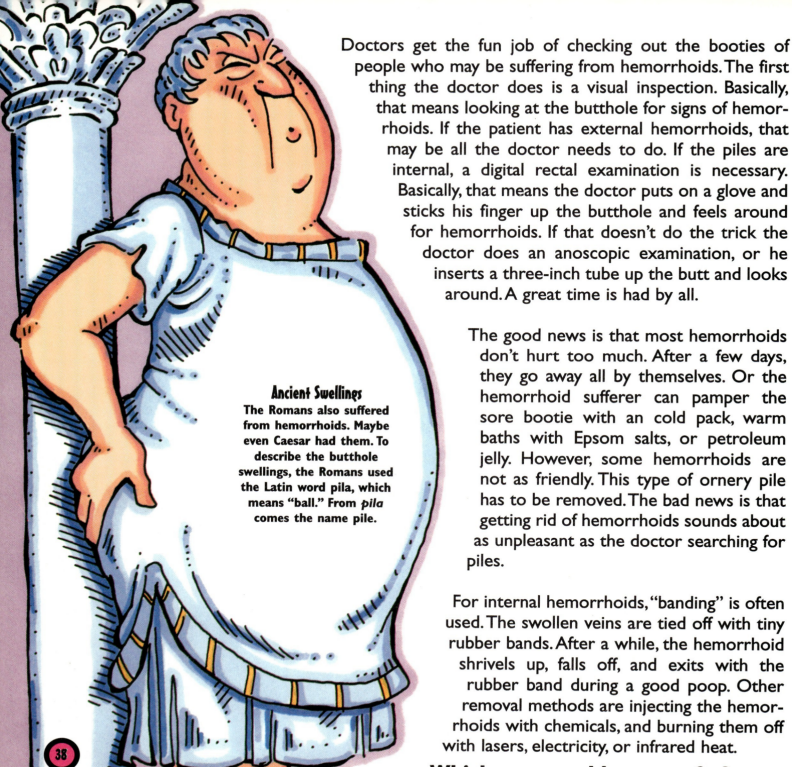

Doctors get the fun job of checking out the booties of people who may be suffering from hemorrhoids. The first thing the doctor does is a visual inspection. Basically, that means looking at the butthole for signs of hemorrhoids. If the patient has external hemorrhoids, that may be all the doctor needs to do. If the piles are internal, a digital rectal examination is necessary. Basically, that means the doctor puts on a glove and sticks his finger up the butthole and feels around for hemorrhoids. If that doesn't do the trick the doctor does an anoscopic examination, or he inserts a three-inch tube up the butt and looks around. A great time is had by all.

The good news is that most hemorrhoids don't hurt too much. After a few days, they go away all by themselves. Or the hemorrhoid sufferer can pamper the sore bootie with an cold pack, warm baths with Epsom salts, or petroleum jelly. However, some hemorrhoids are not as friendly. This type of ornery pile has to be removed. The bad news is that getting rid of hemorrhoids sounds about as unpleasant as the doctor searching for piles.

For internal hemorrhoids, "banding" is often used. The swollen veins are tied off with tiny rubber bands. After a while, the hemorrhoid shrivels up, falls off, and exits with the rubber band during a good poop. Other removal methods are injecting the hemorrhoids with chemicals, and burning them off with lasers, electricity, or infrared heat.

Which one would you prefer?

Ancient Swellings
The Romans also suffered from hemorrhoids. Maybe even Caesar had them. To describe the butthole swellings, the Romans used the Latin word pila, which means "ball." From *pila* comes the name pile.

For external hemorrhoids there is less choice. They can be cut off with a laser or a knife. **No, thanks.**

Avoiding piles is easier than getting them. All you need to do is eat fresh vegetables, fruits, and bran. Also, poop regularly; don't hold it. Finally, don't strain when you drain. In other words, relax when you're perched on the throne.

"Man! As if the entire morning hasn't been gross enough without this." You replace the tube in the cabinet. "I don't even want to know who had to buy this stuff." You ready yourself for a quick face splashing, when you get a whiff of an awful smell.

Sniff, sniff, yuck . . .

Piles of History

The great French emperor Napoleon, conquered much of Europe during the late 1700's and early 1800's. He was remembered mostly for his famous stance of standing with his hand thrust into the open breast buttons of his jacket. Napoleon met his downfall at Waterloo in 1815. Part of his defeat was due to a flare-up of hemorrhoids. Although no medical records exist from that time, accounts of the day suggest that Napoleon had piles and his hemorrhoidal pain impaired his performance at the crucial battle. Napoleon was probably concentrating on his rear, while his troops fell behind in the battle. Talk about a pile of defeat!

Kitty Litter

THE SECRET OF BURIED TREASURE

You stop dead in your tracks. "Yuck." You hear a scratch, scratch from behind. As you turn around, you see Fluffy scurrying from the bathroom after completing his morning bathroom ritual. "Ugh! Why did he have to do it while I was in here?" You look into the kitty toilet. Yep, there it is—a newly laid, half-covered pile of kitty turds.

Humans flush it or leave it behind. Cats are much more particular. They bury it. This really isn't a big deal for cats in the wild. They find a private place, dig a little hole, hunch over, do their duty, sniff it, and bury it with the dirt that's around. Then they wander off until nature calls once again. They find a clean spot and repeat the actions. Even outdoor house cats have an entire neighborhood. They often seek out places with soft soil, like the garden. There, they dig a little kitty dookie hole before relieving themselves, cover it over, then go on their merry way.

It is the indoor kitty that must subject his natural instincts to a human-made solution—the litter box. The litter box solution works just fine for most cats. There are a few rebels who prefer the soil in potted plants or the center of the living room floor. Usually though, if the litter box is kept clean, the renegades can be trained to use it.

Humans spend millions of dollars every year on toiletries for Boots. There is the litter box, the liner, pooper scoopers, and litter.

If You Must Know
House cats pee two to four times a day.

40

The word litter really doesn't seem to fit for this cat ritual. Litter means rubbish or objects scattered in a disordered way. Boots does not toss around his feces, he carefully places them into a hole. Maybe the litter part comes in after Boots is done and he tosses the dirt substitute over his leavings and sometimes all over the floor.

When it comes to setting up Tabby's bathroom, the number of choices is staggering. The first decision is the litter box: Covered or uncovered? Some people think cats would prefer a covered box because it is more private. The problem with hooded poo poo containers is that they are hooded. Out of sight, out of mind. This may mean that Morris is stepping knee deep in doo doo before anyone thinks to change the kitty litter. Actually, by this time Morris is probably pooping on the couch trying to get someone's attention. If you know you will attend carefully to Morris' anal needs, a covered box is great. If not, settle for the plastic open container. Buy a box that is big enough. Otherwise, Morris' butt may hang over the edge when he squats, defeating the reason you bought the thing in the first place.

Hi-Tech Toilet

Computer technology has entered the land of kitty toilets. A self-cleaning kitty litter box is available that senses the dookie and automatically scoops it out. No muss, no fuss, no Muffy. No Muffy? She must have gotten scooped into the dirty litter storage again.

When choosing the perfect litter, keep three qualities in mind: texture, clumpability, and scent. The most important quality to Tiger is the tootsie touch. The texture of the litter must feel good under Tiger's paws or she won't use the box. Litter can be made from wood, clay, wheat hull, recycled paper, earth, or sand. Some people prefer a homemade variety, such as shredded paper or garden soil. *Oh decisions, decisions.* Warning! Once you and Tiger settle on the perfect litter, don't change it. Tiger knows what she likes and she may resort to peeing in the sink if you buy the brand that's on sale.

To clump or not to clump? That is the question if you are human; cats really don't care. Some litters brag that moisture causes their brand to ball up, which makes it easy to remove. Just scoop out the clods of urine instead of changing all of the litter. So, if you're into picking out individual clods from the litter box, go for it.

Finally, there's the smell factor. Some litters contain order-eating chemicals. Yep, and eat odors they will . . . for a short time. If you really don't want a stinky litter box, change it. Every day you should keep Puddytat happy

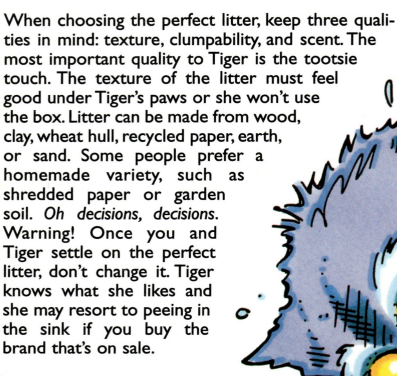

Tabby on the Throne
You can train your cat to do its anal business in the toilet. Yep, there's a little training kit you can buy to help teach your cat to do it. No, Fluffy won't flush after he's finished.

by shoveling out the poops. This is why a pooper scooper is so handy. These amazing inventions look like spatulas with holes. When you capture the poop, the litter drains through the holes. It's kind of like panning for gold.

Once a week, dump out all of the cruddy litter and put in fresh stuff. Pregnant woman and people with immune disorders should not clean out yucky kitty litter trays, as there is a slight chance they could get a disease called toxoplasmosis. Wash out the pan with vinegar or bleach. Many household cleaners could make Flower sick, so don't use them. Also, stuff with ammonia in it will smell like stale pee to your kitty. "Yuck, stale pee. I'm not going in there. I think I'll just use the bed instead." You may want to cover the bottom of the container with newspaper or a liner before laying down fresh litter. If more than one kitty lives in your home, you should change the litter a lot more often.

So, you chose a litter box, liner, scoop, and kitty litter. That's all there is to it. Your nose wrinkles at the wafting air of fresh cat doo doo. "Great, and I haven't even eaten yet."

Oops

A Spanish-speaking woman wandered into a pet store, pointed to the pooper scooper, and tried to ask questions. The clerk did not know how to speak Spanish, so she called a friend on the phone to translate. The Spanish woman left quickly after speaking briefly on the phone. The clerk asked her giggling friend what had happened. Her friend told her that the woman had thought the pooper scoopers were pasta spoons.

Cockroaches

GOOD CLEAN COMPANIONS

You scramble into the kitchen. Time to break the fast, or, in easier words, time to eat breakfast. "Let's see. Super Sugar-Coated Crunchies sound perfect." You open the cupboard.

"**Euwwwww.** A cockroach. How disgusting. Smash it." Scuttle. Scuttle. Gone.

Most humans are amazingly grossed out by cockroaches. But why? *Because they are dirty, of course.* Actually, cockroaches are pretty clean. If a cockroach could talk, it would tell you that humans are the yucky ones. Cockroaches are so repulsed by humans, they often lick themselves clean after a human touch. Roaches spit-shine their antennae by running them through their mouths. Antennae are important because they feel and taste for the roach.

OK, OK, they do poop and pee, but what animal doesn't? Cockroaches can't help it if they do it when the urge hits. You can't train the little buggers to go in the litter box and there aren't diapers small enough for a cockroach. They also can't help it if their droppings and dribblings make a room smell a little musty. Think about a whiff of Muffy's kitty litter box after a few days and cockroach waste doesn't seem so awful. *I would really rather not, thank you.*

If I Only Had a Brain
Cockroaches don't have much for brains because most of their nervous system runs through their body, instead. That's why a cockroach can live for 10 days without a head.

Pee isn't a large portion of the stinky problem for cockroaches, because they don't tinkle much; instead, they store it for hard times. The insect pee, or uric acid, is put away in a part of the cockroach called the "fat body," which is located in this creature's back. A cockroach can live for weeks without food just because of the ability to store its pee. One scientist kept a cockroach colony for two and a half years without feeding the roaches any food protein at all. Cockroaches probably think humans are the dirty ones, and they like it that way.

The Roachiest Cities
Americans spend almost $300 million dollars a year on roach killers. The city that spends the most money on roach-away is Los Angeles, CA. New York City comes in second. Three cities in Texas come in next: Houston, Dallas, and San Antionio.

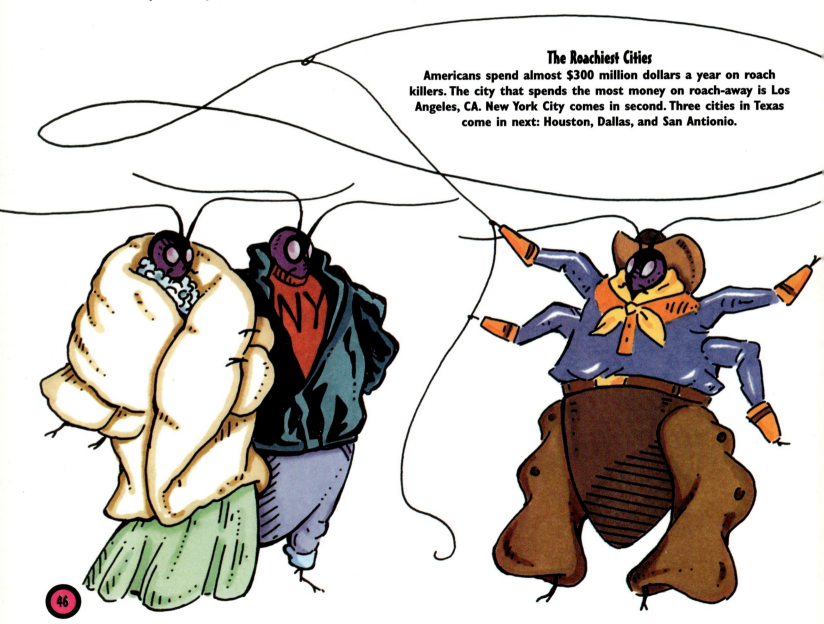

Leftover food bits, overflowing garbage pails, and dirty dishes are yummy time for the roach family. Cockroaches chow down almost anything from grease on a kitchen wall to tennis shoe sweat. They even enjoy dookie treats. But, just like you, cockroaches have their favorite treats. Given a choice, roaches prefer cinnamon rolls, white bread, and boiled potatoes.

Although roaches are not poisonous or dangerous, they might make people sick by spreading germs, or bacteria, as they travel from a taste at the kitty litter box to a lick of the rotting garbage, then to finish off the meal at the fruit bowl on the counter. "Care for a roachy, bacteria-coated apple?" Other cockroach experts claim that the pesky critters only harm people with allergies to cockroaches.

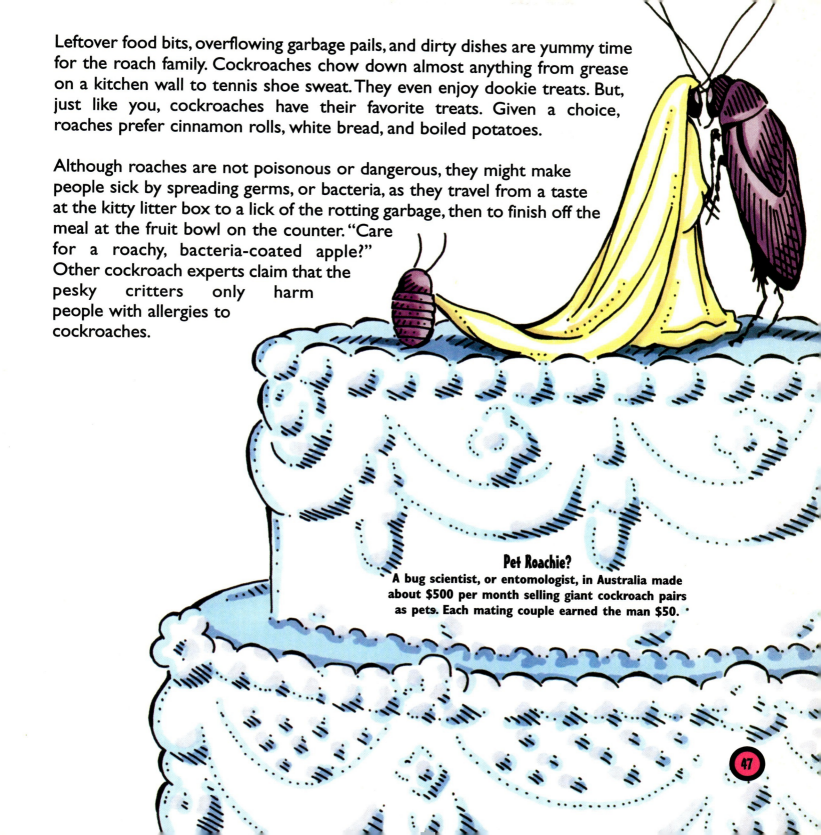

Pet Roachie?
A bug scientist, or entomologist, in Australia made about $500 per month selling giant cockroach pairs as pets. Each mating couple earned the man $50.

Well, roaches aren't that dirty. But they're still putrid. So many of them crawling around. Yep, there are a lot of cockroaches. Over 3,500 different kinds of roaches creep all over the world, except maybe Antarctica. Most of them can't stand humans. They live in caves and under logs. But a few, about 35 different species, really like us—or at least they like our lifestyle. Four types commonly hang out in diners and kitchens during the after-hours. The German cockroach (although the Germans call it the French cockroach) has even hitched rides on airplanes. The Oriental cock-roach, also incorrectly called the black beetle, is about an inch long and shiny black. The American cockroach likes restaurants, bakeries, and grocery stores. The brown-banded cockroach flies readily. Other types of cockroaches include . . .

Big and Talkative
The Madagascar hissing cockroach is as big as a mouse. Yes, it actually hisses.

Stop
Light

*Stop right there. I meant so many in number, not in
kinds. Like they hang out in large cockroach gangs.* Yep, the
roaches are very social. The lone cockroach would not be a
hero among the cockies. Guess you could say, if you've seen one,
you haven't seen them all. The German cockroaches ooze a chemical that
draws the roaches together in a crowd. The Asian roaches really throw a party.
Thousands of these flying cockroaches will gather on a wall. On the ground a group
of 30 may form a roach cluster. SQUISH! Crunnnnnnnch. Thirty in one step. Lovely
cockroach goo on your shoe.

Even if only a couple of cockroach drifters make their way into, say, your cereal cupboard, there
won't be two for very long. That is, if the couple is a male and a female. If they were German
cockroaches, after a year your cupboard would be overrun with 500,000 of the creatures.
If the couple were Asian cockroaches, 10 million roaches would overtake
your entire kitchen. That would be more roaches in your kitchen
alone than all of the people in New York City. "Mom, who ate
all of the cookies?"

Cockroaches existed on Earth before the dinosaurs were here. They are one of the most successful animals because they can adjust to most anything. Basically, that means they are really hard for humans to get rid of. The poisons that kill the critters can also harm us, so they have to be used carefully.

The best way to keep away cockroaches is to clean, clean, clean and to keep an area dry. If that doesn't work, you could try capturing the critters and selling them as great house pets.

I may know more about cockroaches but they are still disgusting. Can't win them all.

You close the cupboard, leaving the cereal for another day. "That roach must have free-loaded in with yesterday's groceries." You head toward the refrigerator. "Milk and toast should be safe."

The Living Roach Motel

WHAT YOU NEED:

A cockroach or two, paper plate, petroleum jelly, large jar with holes in the lid, small bowl, water, various foods.

WHAT YOU DO:

First you need to catch some cockroaches. Smear a layer of petroleum jelly over the plate. Add some yummy food to the plate, such as white bread or cinnamon rolls. Find a roachy area. If you don't have any at home, try behind a diner or near a stack of wood. Be careful not to announce your plan inside of the diner, as the customers would prefer to enjoy their meal. While you wait, prepare your roach's new home. Poke holes in the lid of a jar. Place a small bowl of water in the jar. You may also want to decorate the home with sticks or cardboard hiding spots. Check the roach traps in the morning. After you catch a cockroach, place it in the jar. Let it get adjusted. You will know your new friend is calm when it slows down. Name your cockroach friend. Try feeding your cockroach various types of food to find out which it prefers. Treat your cockroach kindly and don't let it out in the house.

Rotten Food

IS NOT JUST WHAT YOU THINK IT IS

You grab a loaf of bread and remove a slice. While placing it in the toaster, you notice something weird. Little dots of blue-green peek at you from the surface of the slice.

"Uck, the bread is moldy."

Upon closer inspection, you notice the furry mat along the top of the bread. Ack, it's all rotten. You dump the woolly slices in the compost.

A clean glass awaits your cold milk. You open the cardboard milk container and pour. "Whoa!" Your nose curls up. You notice clumps of curdled milk plopping into the glass. "As if things weren't gross enough already."

Wee beasties called bacteria are everywhere. So what stops the hungry critters from settling on your food? Nothing. Well, almost nothing. Really hot or really cold food is not their cup of tea. Also they prefer to dine on meats and dairy products. Vegetarians they are not.

Food left out can easily fall prey to bacteria. The bacteria munch on the food. After a short while, your chicken is teeming with the little animals. You place the chicken in the refrigerator. The cold slows down their growth. You remove the chicken after several days, open the container and take a whiff. Yuck. The rancid smell makes you want to puke. Actually, this is good because your body is telling you that you don't want to eat the stuff. Instead of throwing up, you throw out the chicken in the garbage. The bacteria keep on munching away.

You say that the food is spoiled. However, for a hunk of meat on the ground, spoiling is good. The bacteria help the food to rot or decompose. This returns the meat to the soil. And that is good.

But in your home, it is not so great. If you accidentally take a bite of the bacteria-filled chicken, you could get really sick. This is called food poisoning. You could yell at the bacteria, "Hey, you creeps. Stay away from my food." But this won't do much good.

Bacteria don't have ears.

Bye, Bye Bready
Every year in the United States several million dollars worth of bread is thrown out because it is moldy.

53

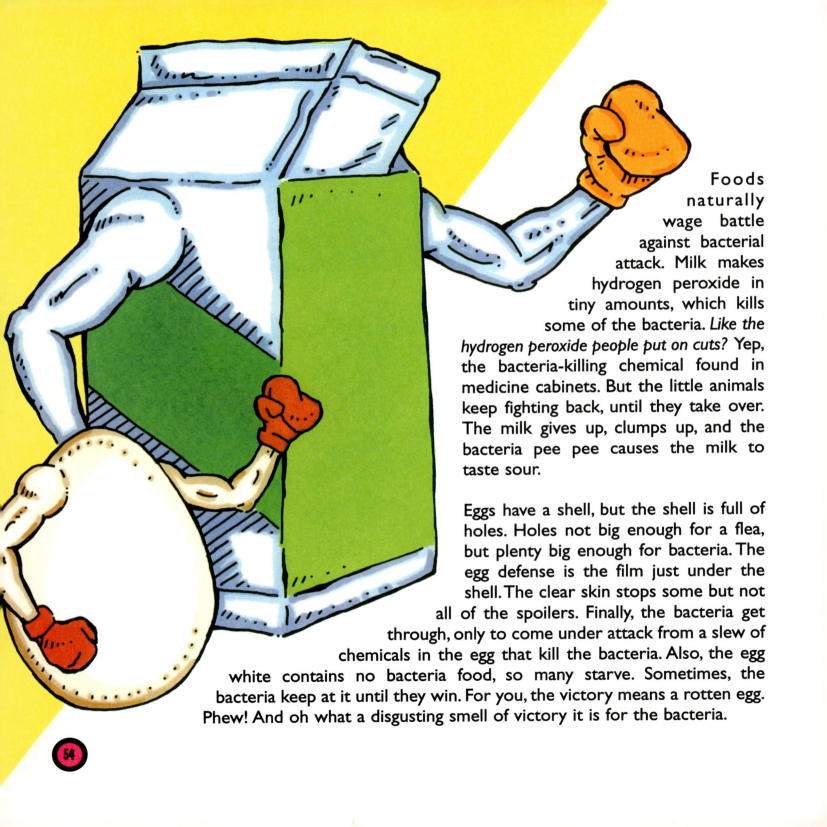

Foods naturally wage battle against bacterial attack. Milk makes hydrogen peroxide in tiny amounts, which kills some of the bacteria. *Like the hydrogen peroxide people put on cuts?* Yep, the bacteria-killing chemical found in medicine cabinets. But the little animals keep fighting back, until they take over. The milk gives up, clumps up, and the bacteria pee pee causes the milk to taste sour.

Eggs have a shell, but the shell is full of holes. Holes not big enough for a flea, but plenty big enough for bacteria. The egg defense is the film just under the shell. The clear skin stops some but not all of the spoilers. Finally, the bacteria get through, only to come under attack from a slew of chemicals in the egg that kill the bacteria. Also, the egg white contains no bacteria food, so many starve. Sometimes, the bacteria keep at it until they win. For you, the victory means a rotten egg. Phew! And oh what a disgusting smell of victory it is for the bacteria.

Humans have waged war against bacteria for a long time. Foods are pasteurized, or heated. The heat kills the bacteria. Then the food is put into cans or other clean containers. This works great as long is the container is not open or dented. Once the germless food is exposed to the air, the bacteria move right in. Basically, the bacteria win the battle of spoiled food over and over.

And if that's not enough, there are the little woolly friends of rot called **fungi (FUN jeye)**. Right now you can easily find some lurking about your house. Try the moldings around the shower or the forgotten soda by your bed. How about the pile of wood in your yard?

Even better, check out the cheese drawer in your refrigerator. There's a chance you have eaten some for dinner. *Ick!* And liked it. If you have ever enjoyed blue cheese, you've eaten fungi. Soy sauce is made from these critters too. Finally, there is the very obvious mushroom that may lay upon your slice of pizza or hide on your salad.

Yep, fungi.

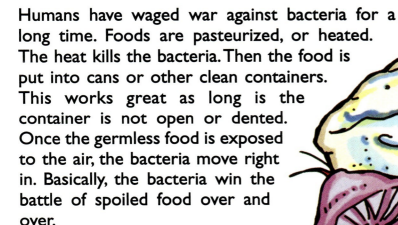

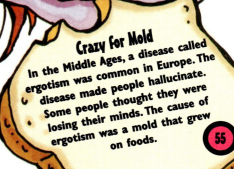

Crazy for Mold
In the Middle Ages, a disease called ergotism was common in Europe. The disease made people hallucinate. Some people thought they were losing their minds. The cause of ergotism was a mold that grew on foods.

55

You might know these spoilers and rotters better as molds, mildews, blights, rot, smuts, rusts, and mushrooms. Together this group of decomposers is known as fungi. The gang also includes yeast. It is a very determined group that lives most anywhere from bathroom tile to grapes to paint. Fungi are amazing decomposers. If it weren't for fungi, the world would be covered in dead stuff as high as your ceiling. So, the next time you wander outside, thank a fungus.

The problem with fungi is also what is so right about them. They help to make things rot. Since fungi can't be trained when to rot and when not to rot, they move right in on the food that you planned to eat.

Right now there are probably little fungus eggs floating around your house. Actually, they aren't called eggs at all, they are called spores. The teeny tiny little baby fungus balls float around until they land on something that they can decompose. Depending upon the type of fungus, the great food could be bread, orange peels, grease on the wall, or paint in the bathroom. Fungi are so diverse, they can even feed on gasoline.

Go Figure

The world mildew had its origins from an old English word "meledeaw," which meant honeydew. How the word came to refer to the moldy stuff in the refrigerator is anybody's guess. Maybe lots of mildew grew on honeydew melons? Or maybe honeydew melons were named after the mold?

More Mold, Please!

Check out your vitamin C tablets and your fake lemonade for an ingredient called citric acid. Nope, the flavoring probably doesn't comes from lemons. It is made by a black mold.

56

Once they land, the moldy type put out little branches called **hyphae (HIGH fee)**. The little branches grow until a mat of mold forms. That's when you first notice little green, brown, white, or black spots. Given enough time and yummy food, the mold gets furrier and larger. Bread molds actually mate. They then form little stalks with big puffy heads, or fruiting bodies. The heads burst open and spew spores into the air.

Mostly, molds and mildews don't hurt us, except for people who are allergic to the spores. The tiny spores cause some people to sneeze and complain. Being allergic to the spores isn't very pleasant, especially since the little creatures live most everywhere.

If you ever tasted moldy food, it tastes . . . well, it tastes moldy, which isn't too pleasant.

However, one special type of mold is the unique flavor for blue cheese. The blue you see in blue cheese is mold. Yep, if weren't for **Penicillin roquefortii**, there would be many unhappy salad eaters. A cousin of the same type of mold is even responsible for saving million of lives. The drug penicillin is produced by the same green mold that disgusts you when it grows on an orange or bread. The wonder drug was even named in the honor of the mold that makes it. Hooray for molds!

Other great fungi in history include yeast. This fungus makes bread. No, it isn't the one that makes bread moldy: it is the one that makes bread rise. Yeast loves warmth and sugar. A bit of the dried creatures are added to bread dough. The sugar or starch in the bread along with the warm water brings the yeast back to life. The happy little fungi munch away. As they eat, they fart out carbon dioxide, which makes the bread rise. They also make waste. Only yeast waste is not urea like the stuff in human pee. It is alcohol. (Yep, alcohol is a sort of yeast pee.) The alcohol in the bread evaporates as the bread bakes. The yeast all die from the very warm temperatures as well. *Oooooh, poor little yeasties.*

The fungus among us add all sorts of variety to life. So, the next time you see the scum in the refrigerator, remember don't judge a fungus by its brother.

"OK, OK, the fungus and the bacteria can have my milk and toast." You sit down at the table. "Enough is enough. But I can't starve. There must be something I can eat."

Your Oral Planet

If you were to just scrape the saliva off of your tongue, you would collect over 50 million tiny creatures. Lovely. Actually, you have more creatures in your mouth than there are people living on Earth.

Moldy Bread and Sour Milk

WHAT YOU NEED:

Two slices of bread, two resealable plastic bags, water, milk, one cup, two small jars, refrigerator.

WHAT YOU DO:

To find out where bread mold grows best, choose a dark spot and a bright spot. Place a slice of bread in each bag. If you want lots of mold and maybe other stuff, rub each slice in a dusty area before placing in the bag. Dip your fingers into some water and sprinkle the water onto each slice of bread. Don't soak the bread, just make it damp. Close the bag. Place one bag with bread in a dark area and place the other bag with bread in a light area. After five or so days, check each bag. Which bag was home to the most furry friends? Discard the bags with the moldy bread after you show them to your great aunt.

To find out which temperature makes bacteria sour milk faster, choose a safe spot in the refrigerator and a safe spot in a warm place. Pour a glass of milk. Leave the glass of milk out for several hours, or until the milk warms to room temperature. Pour half of the milk into one jar, cover, and place the jar in a secure spot in the refrigerator. Pour the rest of the milk into the other jar and put the jar in the safe warm place. Check the milk after several days. You may want to leave the jars even longer, if your mother will let you. After a week or so, how does the milk look? Smelling the milk probably isn't a good idea at this point. Discard the jars after they become too disgusting for words.

Food Invaders

SOMETHING BUGGING YOU?

You finally settle for a muffin and orange juice. You read the label on the side of the orange juice can—oranges, water. Sounds edible and not gross at all. You think of the cockroach in the cupboard, the bacteria and mold in the rotten food. "I'm so glad I don't eat anything disgusting."

Over 1,000 different types of bugs are eaten by cultures throughout the world. In parts of Mexico, Africa, and Asia, insects such as water bugs, locusts, termites, ants, and grubs are common foods.

OK, so your mouth doesn't water when you see a fat grub in the garden. And you don't dash for a frying pan to collect ants crawling in your yard. You may even say, "No bugs ever pass between these lips."

But the gross fact is, you eat many bugs and bug parts without knowing it. Most foods have insect contaminates.

Ack! Tell the health inspectors! Well, those people already know, and they even allow a set number of bugs, bug parts, and rodent contaminants in foods. These amounts are called DALs or food Defect Action Levels.

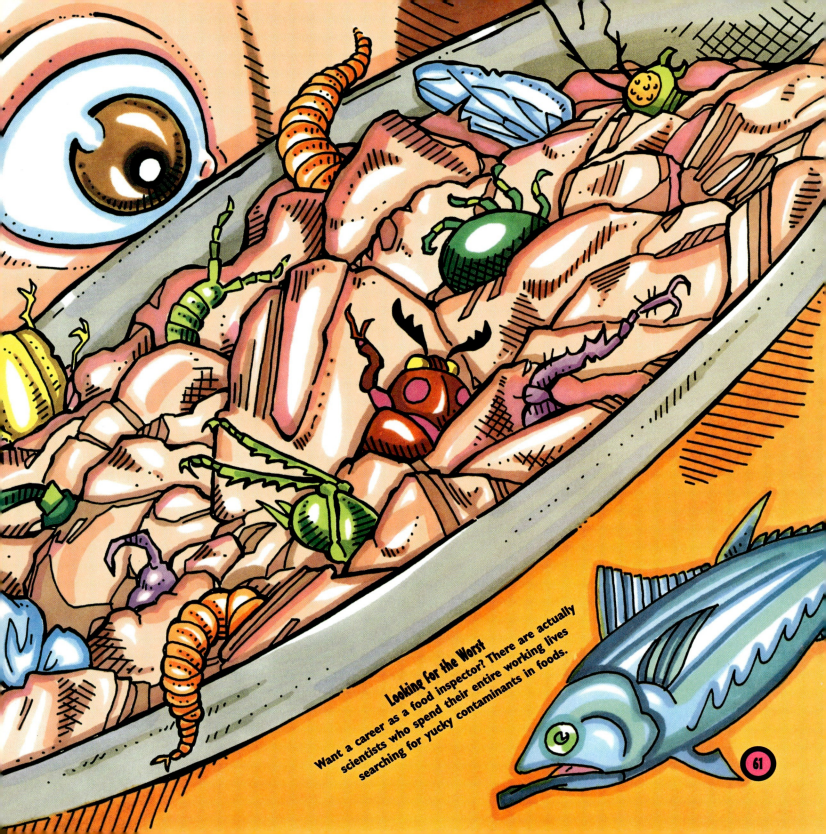

Looking for the Worst
Want a career as a food inspector? There are actually scientists who spend their entire working lives searching for yucky contaminants in foods.

61

Let's say that this is your diet for one day. According to the DALs, you could be eating the following.

Breakfast bug intake: In six cornbread muffins—four whole insects, 200 insect fragments, and four rodent poops are allowed. In a 12-ounce glass of canned orange juice—1.5 maggots. In a one-pound jar of apple butter—18 rodent hairs and 22 insects.

Time for lunch!

Your peanut butter and raspberry preserves on wheat bread (in one pound of peanut butter—150 insect fragments and five rodent hairs; in a 24-ounce jar of preserves—10 whole insects; in three and a half cups of wheat flour—125 insect fragments and three rodent hairs) tastes great!

 Oh yes, there's the 90-insect-fragment, three-rodent-hairs, medium-size chocolate bar.

Bet you can't wait for your spaghetti dinner! *I think I lost my appetite.*

Your bug allowance for spaghetti is three maggots in a large can of tomatoes, 45 fly eggs and three maggots in a 12-ounce can of tomato paste, and 45 small maggots and 169 mites in the eight-ounce can of mushrooms. Dump that over one-half pound of noodles with about 200 insect fragments and four rodent hairs. Have some frozen broccoli with it: 140 whole aphids, thripes, or mites.

No dessert tonight? What a pity.

An Earthy Meal

Maggot paté, grasshopper guacamole, and, for dessert—earthworm and applesauce cake. That was the menu for a bug feast offered by an **entomology (ent a MOLL oh gee)** professor at the University of California at Berkeley. (Entomologists study insects.)

According to Don, who actually attended the feast and even ate it without tossing his cookies, "The maggot paté tastes kind of like chicken. The maggots were ground, but it still had that maggot color. Actually, it's not too bad if you don't think about wriggling little worms in your garbage."

Don said the earthworms weren't really noticeable in the cake, especially if you didn't look closely. His least favorite was the grasshopper guacamole. "The grasshoppers were chopped up, but it had a strange crunch that didn't seem right for guacamole."

Obviously, the contaminants are spread throughout the can or bag of food, so your helping doesn't get it all. However, for grossness purposes, say that every serving you ate for the entire day has the highest number of allowable contaminants. Your intake for the day would be 52.5 maggots, 355 whole bugs, 765 insect fragments, 45 fly eggs, 33 rodent hairs, and four rodent poops. Never eat bugs, huh?

"Well, what's a kid to do?" You take the last bite of your muffin and wash it down with the orange juice. Then you smack your lips loudly, as your stomach turns.

THERE'S A FLY IN YOUR SOUP (MAYBE MORE)...

YUMMY FOOD...
ALLOWABLE
CONTAMINANTS:

FROZEN ASPARAGUS
1 lb. bag
22 any size whole insects

Recipes for the Brave
Don't know how to whip up a tasty centipede casserole or chocolate-covered ants? Not to worry. There are cookbooks available that specialize in fixing yummy insect treats.

GOLDEN RAISINS
8 oz. box
10 insects
35 fruit fly eggs

TOMATO JUICE
Small can
1.5 maggots
7.5 fly eggs

POPCORN

1 lb. bag
2 rodent hairs

FROZEN SPINACH

1 lb. bag
225 aphids or thrips or mites

FROZEN BRUSSELS SPROUTS

1 lb. bag
135 aphids or thrips

COCOA POWDER

8 oz. can
562 insect fragments
18 rodent hairs

65

Kitchen Germs

BEWARE THE SPONGE

The wrenching in your stomach settles to a mild queasiness. You notice the crumbs left behind on the table. From the kitchen sink, you grab the sponge. "Yes, just wipe it. Keep it clean and it won't be so putrid."

When you use a sponge to wipe the table, you just **think** you clean the table. OK, you actually do remove bread crumbs and drops of gravy. But you also deposit millions of wee beasties in their place.

The tiny bacteria bathe in the wetness of the sponge or the dish cloth. The tiny critters are deposited with the water in the cloth where you wipe. Even if you look **reallllly** close, you can't see them. The little one-celled animals are so small that thousands of them in a pile would not even be as big as the period at the end of this sentence. But don't let their small size fool you. They are alive! They make things stink and some types can even make you sick.

And now they are all over your table. And if you wiped the counter, they are there, too. And the refrigerator handle, and the front of the cupboard, and the cutting board, and your little sister's face, and . . . well, you get the point.

The bacteria wiggle upon the table and try to stay away from dangerous objects like giant landing plates and falling newspapers. They don't have feet to walk or wings to fly. The cigar-shaped creatures, called **Pseudomonas,** move by using a single whiplike tail or many whiplike tails. The tails are called **flagella (fla GEL a)**. A wiggle of the flagella swishes the bacteria across your "clean" counter or table top. Some types of bacteria are shaped like little balls; other have a sausage shape. These types can't scoot out of harm's way. Once the table dries, the bacteria die out after a couple of hours. But by then, you probably wiped the surface again, giving your table friends the moisture they need to survive.

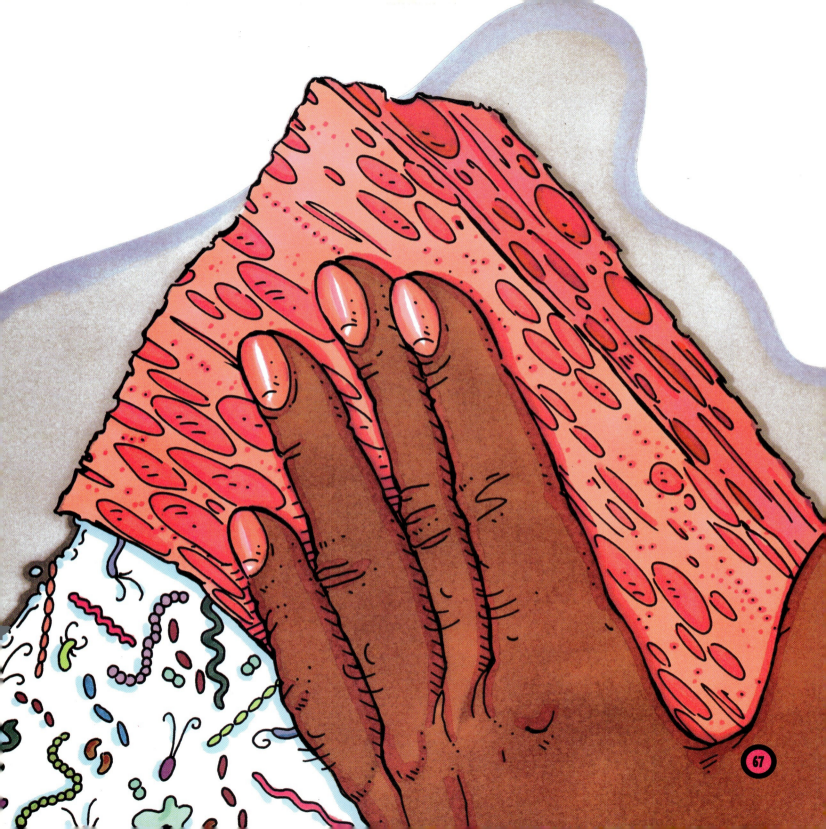

Sponges and dishrags are great places for the bacteria because they can attach to the surface, they can eat the teensy tiny bits of food, and they love moisture. "Yes, dear. It's everything we always wanted." The bacteria move in. They set up housekeeping and start reproducing. In the liquid from one wrung-out sponge, scientists have found over 10 million bacteria. That's a lot when you consider there are about nine million people in the entire state of Michigan.

The happy creatures and their offspring hang out as long the dishrag is damp. You can tell if the bacteria are happy by smelling the dishrag or sponge. **No, thank you**. Rancid dishrags and sponges are a sure sign of contented bacteria living, eating, pooping, and mating in their little sponge world. If the sponge dries out, they die off in several days.

Ahhhhhh, how sad.

Well, it's really not so tragic if you have wiped your cutting board, because some of them left the sponge world and moved to the cutting board world. Bacteria love cutting boards because they can hang out in the knife scars. On plastic boards, the bacteria hang out on the surface, so the germs are more likely to spread to your foods. This can really be a problem because some types of bacteria cause food poisoning. On wooden boards, they hide out in the wood pores below the surface, so they don't spread as easily.

Yipes, enough already.
I am not ever eating again.

Dinner in the John?
Your bathroom is probably a cleaner place to eat than your kitchen. A group of scientists found that most toilet seats have less bacteria than your kitchen sink.

69

Hey, it's not that hopeless. People have eaten in kitchens for a long time. The key to stopping bacteria from over-running your life is to keep stuff fresh and clean.

Don't leave damp rags and sponges around. Wring them out. Wash them often. Getting rid of bacteria from pans is isn't too difficult either.

Pans? They live on metal too? There's no escape.

Keep out the bacteria in the first place by scrubbing well, using hot water, and keeping the surface dry. The same is true for cutting boards. Wash the board after each use. Don't cut up chicken and then use the same dirty board for cutting tomatoes. Wash it well after each type of food. Dishwashers and microwaves are also helpful.

Sponges at Fault
Scientists studying bacteria in homes discovered one kitchen where the germs were spread everywhere. On the sixth day, the kitchen was suddenly germ-free. Upon further investigation, it turned out the family had started using a new sponge.

Grow Your Own Bacteria

WHAT YOU NEED:

Chicken bullion cube, water, measuring cup, sugar, three very clean bowls, spoon, pan, plastic wrap, one packet of gelatin (optional).

WHAT YOU DO:

Measure three cups of water into a pan. Distilled water works best, but tap water is OK. Bring the water to a boil. Add the bullion cube and one spoonful of sugar to the water. Allow the mixture to boil for several minutes. After several minutes, cover the pan and remove it from the heat. Now get out three very, very clean bowls (if you are using gelatin, add it to the bullion mixture at this time). Pour equal amounts of the bullion mixture into each bowl. You should have a little less than one cup in each bowl.

Pick three different spots to place a bowl. On the back of the toilet seat, near the garbage, or by the kitchen sink are good spots. Or try coughing in one bowl, dabbing your fingers in another bowl, and leaving one alone. Once you have readied your bowls for bacteria, leave them out for one day. After one day, cover the bowls with plastic wrap and place them in a secure and warm place. Allow your bacteria friends to grow for a week. Then check to see what has grown.

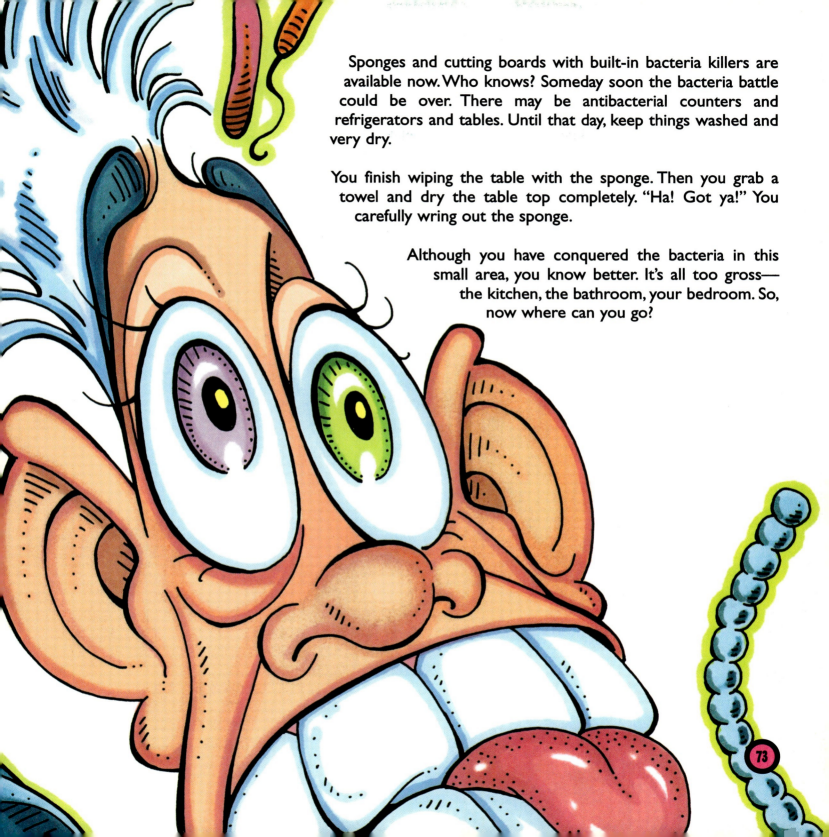

Sponges and cutting boards with built-in bacteria killers are available now. Who knows? Someday soon the bacteria battle could be over. There may be antibacterial counters and refrigerators and tables. Until that day, keep things washed and very dry.

You finish wiping the table with the sponge. Then you grab a towel and dry the table top completely. "Ha! Got ya!" You carefully wring out the sponge.

Although you have conquered the bacteria in this small area, you know better. It's all too gross—the kitchen, the bathroom, your bedroom. So, now where can you go?

Kissing

THE SPITTY NITTY-GRITTY

You flee to the living room, a safe place. You plunk yourself on the couch and grab the comforting remote control. Yes, television, the ultimate escape from the revolting world. At last, some relief from the many gross events of the day. You watch a predictable Hollywood moment—a couple alone on the grassy park knoll satisfied after a picnic lunch, birds singing, no ants, she lies next to him. He leans close to her. She opens her eyes, smiles, and parts her lips slightly. As he approaches her anxious mouth, he is CURSED with microscopic vision. His magnifying eyes glimpse into her mouth.

Argggggh! It's alive in there. Millions of tiny creatures scoot about her spit-soaked teeth, tongue, and cheeks.

"Maybe it will be an interesting scene after all."

Kissing is supposed to be a good thing, right? If it were gross, why would anyone do it? Well, maybe people just don't realize what really happens when a wet and slobbery smooch gets exhanged. That picnic guy on the TV, though, is cursed with microscopic vision so he can see all the teensy tiny stuff in his girlfriend's mouth. Ack! How awful. Hey, what could be inside a mouth anyway?

He looks in horror at the critters on her teeth, tongue, and cheeks. Some of them are spherical, some rod-shaped, and some spiral like curly French fries. They crawl and swim to the micro-tonnage of food particles left behind in her orifice. Bits of cheese and rye bread cling to her white enamel teeth. Banana scum coats her tongue. **Oh gross!** There's even Corn Flake chunks still there from breakfast. And the creatures munch on the leftovers. Then they dribble acid waste. The corrosive acid eats away at her teeth to create cavities.

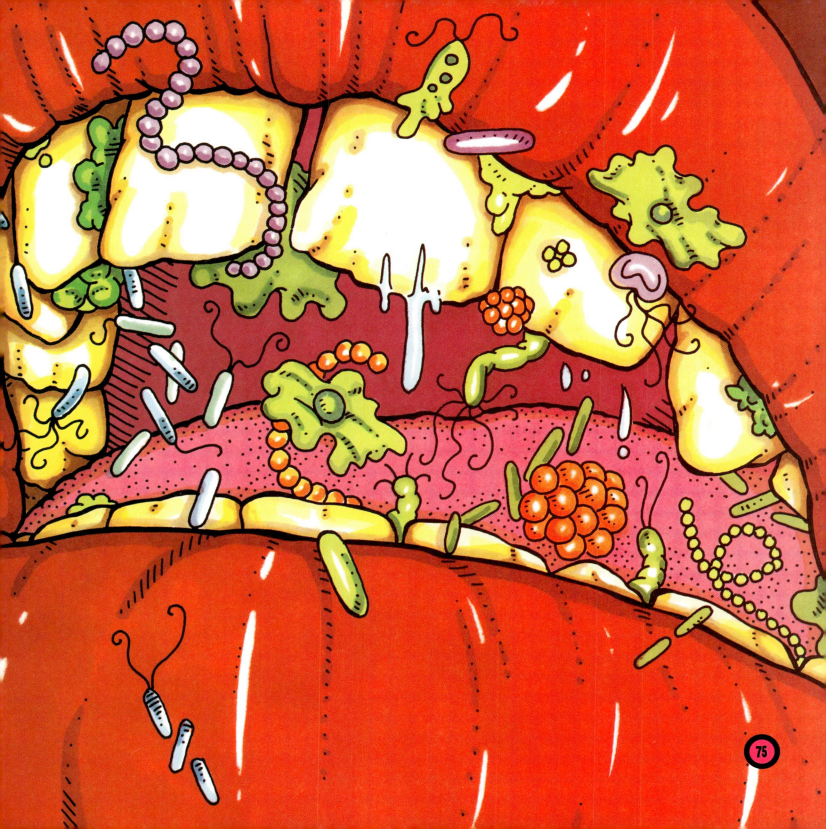

Yeeow! There's even a war going on her mouth. White blood cells creep along like pom poms come to life. Long strands stretch from the round mass to capture and gobble up the bacteria. It's like a late night horror film. **All right, my kind of movie.**

And it's not over. Her mouth— just like anyone's mouth— is home to fungus, or mold, and to viruses. Viruses cause colds and flus. What kind of diseases are hanging out in that mouth?

Upon closer inspection, there's yellow crusty stuff between and around the base of her not pearly whites but crusty yellows. She has tartar, or the stony yellow stuff that densists so love to scrape away. She probably hasn't seen a dentist in several years.

"What are you waiting for?" she asks.

He turns off the microscopic vision by closing his eyes and gently places his dirty, bacteria-filled, food-polluted mouth over hers. Then inserts his tongue into her tartar-laden, germful, food-stuffed mouth. Hey, humans do anything for love.

"OK that's it. I have had it!" You turn off the TV. As you grab your coat from the closet, you spy your big brother kissing his girlfriend in the kitchen. You almost gag.

Puckercise
You burn up about .012 calories every time you kiss someone. Considering you burn up about 300 calories for an hour of walking, smooching isn't too high on the exercise scale. Maybe if you walked and kissed at the same time?

Ten Reasons Why You Shouldn't Kiss Anyone Except Your Dog

1. More than 100,000,000,000 critters live in a human mouth.
2. Bacteria hang out there.
3. Fungus grows in the oral cavity.
4. You might get poked by braces.
5. Mouths have viruses that may cause disease.
6. The white blood cells from someone else's spit will attack in your mouth.
7. You don't want to eat someone else's leftover food bits.
8. Yellow teeth tartar is sickening.
9. Everyone's spit contains a little bit of urinelike stuff from their glands.
10. Acids made by bacteria swish around a mouth.

Dog mouths are more sanitary than human mouths.
Rover's saliva contains enzymes, or chemicals, that kill germs.
Stick to kissing your dog.

Quickly you throw on your coat
and head to the great, clean,
fresh, and pure outdoors.

Or so you think . . .

More Amazing Books from Planet Dexter

GROSSOLOGY
The Science of Really Gross Things!
by Sylvia Branzei

Yup, it's slimy, oozy, stinky, smelly stuff explained. *Grossology* features the gag-rageous science behind the body's most disgusting functions: burps, vomit, scabs, ear wax, you name it. Who could ask for anything more?

ANIMAL GROSSOLOGY™
The Science of All Creatures Gross and Disgusting
by Sylvia Branzei

The author of Planet Dexter's best-selling *Grossology* returns, with this often stomach-turning book about animal life. Find out how a fly eats (yikes!), how to learn from an owl pellet, why a hagfish is so slimy, what the deal is with leeches, and much more.

VIRTUAL GROSSOLOGY
See It! Touch It! Hear It! Smell It! Taste It?
by Sylvia Branzei

Take the original *Grossology* that has won hearts and turned stomachs across the nation, add scratch-n'-sniff and soundboard technology, and what do you get? *Virtual Grossology*, a multi-sensory experience that lets you touch the vomit, hear the belches, and smell the armpits (phew!). A must-have for any grossologist's collection.